NATIONAL
GEOGRAPHIC

Animals All Together

Dominic Loughrey

Four otters sit on the rocks.

Two otters swim in the water.

How many otters all together?
4 + 2 =

Six zebras run across the grass.

Six zebras drink from the river.

How many zebras all together?
6 + 6 =

One whale swims in the sea.

Five whales jump out of the water.

How many whales all together?
$$1 + 5 =$$

Six penguins walk in the snow.

Three penguins dive off the ice.

How many penguins all together?

$$6 + 3 =$$

Five elephants walk on the grass.

Six elephants drink from the river.

How many elephants all together?
5 + 6 =

Animals All Together

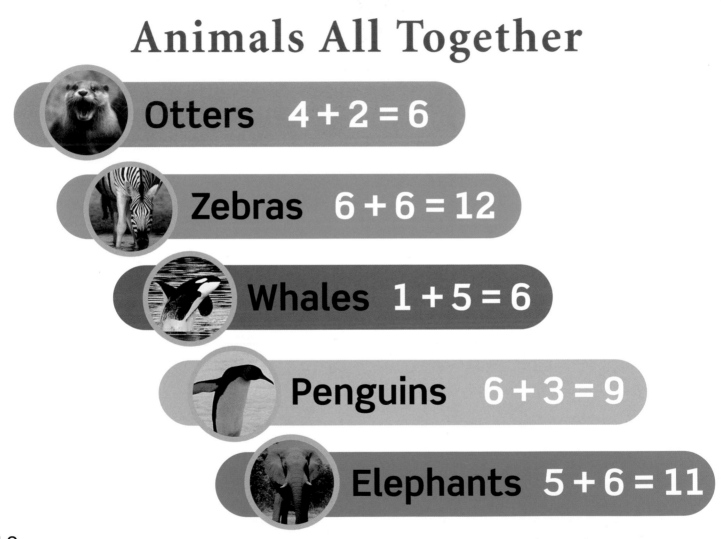

Otters $4 + 2 = 6$

Zebras $6 + 6 = 12$

Whales $1 + 5 = 6$

Penguins $6 + 3 = 9$

Elephants $5 + 6 = 11$